KT-368-122

THE REAL DEAL
Moving

NORWICH CITY COLLEGE

Stock No.	242 689	
Class	648.9 DEG	
Cat.	B2	Proc. 3WL

Terri DeGezelle

Heinemann
LIBRARY

www.heinemann.co.uk/library

Visit our website to find out more information about Heinemann Library books.

To order:

☎ Phone 44 (0) 1865 888066

📠 Send a fax to 44 (0) 1865 314091

💻 Visit the Raintree bookshop at www.heinemann.co.uk/library to browse our catalogue and order online.

Heinemann Library is an imprint of **Pearson Education Limited**, a company incorporated in England and Wales having its registered office at Edinburgh Gate, Harlow, Essex, CM20 2JE – Registered company number: 00872828

Heinemann is a registered trademark of Pearson Education Ltd.

Text © Pearson Education Limited 2009
First published in hardback in 2009
The moral rights of the proprietor have been asserted.

All rights reserved. No part of this publication may be reproduced in any form or by any means (including photocopying or storing it in any medium by electronic means and whether or not transiently or incidentally to some other use of this publication) without the written permission of the copyright owner, except in accordance with the provisions of the Copyright, Designs and Patents Act 1988 or under the terms of a licence issued by the Copyright Licensing Agency, Saffron House, 6–10 Kirby Street, London EC1N 8TS (www.cla.co.uk). Applications for the copyright owner's written permission should be addressed to the publisher.

Edited by Kristen Truhlar, Rachel Howells, and Louise Galpine
Designed by Richard Parker and Manhattan Design
Picture research by Mica Brancic
Production: Victoria Fitzgerald

Originated by Chroma Graphics (Overseas) Pte. Ltd
Printed and bound in China by Leo Paper Group.

ISBN 978 0 431 90808 3 (hardback)
13 12 11 10 09
10 9 8 7 6 5 4 3 2 1

British Library Cataloguing in Publication Data
DeGezelle, Terri, 1955-
Moving. - (The real deal)
155.9'4

A full catalogue record for this book is available from the British Library.

Acknowledgements
We would like to thank the following for permission to reproduce photographs: ©Alamy pp. **4** (Jeff Greenberg), **13** (Ed Maynard), **24** (Janine Wiedel Photolibrary), **26** (Photofusion Picture Library), **27** (Chris Rout); ©Camera Press p. **11**; ©Corbis pp. **9**, **22** (Moodboard), **10** (Nicole Katano/Brand X), **15** (Zave Smith), **18** (Charles Gullung/Zefa), **25** (Erin Ryan/Zefa); ©Getty Images pp. **8**, **20** (Taxi), **16**, **21** (Stone); ©Jupiter Images pp. **5** (Image Source Black), **6** (Workbook Stock), **7** (BananaStock), **12** (Polka Dot Images), **14**; ©Retna p. **19** (Jupiter Images/Blend Images); ©Rex Features p. **23** (Image Source).

Cover photograph of a house for sale sign reproduced with permission of ©Corbis Royalty Free; cover photograph of house keys reproduced with permission of ©iStockphoto/bluestocking.

We would like to thank Anne E. Pezalla for her invaluable help in the preparation of this book.

Every effort has been made to contact copyright holders of any material reproduced in this book. Any omissions will be rectified in subsequent printings if notice is given to the publishers.

Disclaimer
All the Internet addresses (URLs) given in this book were valid at the time of going to press. However, due to the dynamic nature of the Internet, some addresses may have changed, or sites may have changed or ceased to exist since publication. While the author and publishers regret any inconvenience this may cause readers, no responsibility for any such changes can be accepted by either the author or the publishers. It is recommended that adults supervise children on the Internet.

Contents

Some words are printed in bold, **like this**. You can find out what they mean by looking in the glossary.

What is moving?

Packing up belongings, leaving friends behind, and moving to a different location can be upsetting. Moving into a new house, decorating a new bedroom, and making new friends can be exciting. Moving can be a rollercoaster of emotions.

Moving can be difficult, but knowing what to expect can help. Moving can be a **stressful** time for everyone, even for parents. Family members need to talk about their feelings with each other. Moving is a time of change, and change is not always easy.

Families move for many different reasons. Millions of people pack up their belongings and move every year. Some moves include changes in **cultures**, languages, or **climates**.

NEWSFLASH

Job opportunities (new jobs or job transfers) are the top reason for long-distance moves to other counties or countries. The leading reason for moving within the same area is the opportunity to own a house and no longer rent.

Some families move from one country to another, while other families just move within the same local area.

History of moving

Since the beginning of time, people from all areas of the world have moved from one place to another. They moved looking for food, new land, and freedom. Throughout time many people have been forced to move because of **famines**, wars, and overcrowding.

In ancient times, people moved to conquer new lands and increase the size of their kingdoms. They were **attracted** to certain areas because of forests, plentiful food, rivers, and fertile farmland. As lands were discovered, people moved to live in new places.

Centuries later, people packed up and set off looking for a place to start a new life. Families travelled across the ocean from Europe to the United States. Once there, people began moving westwards across the United States. They were searching for land to build a home on and raise a family.

Today, families are on the move around the world. People may move to a different house in the same neighbourhood or to another part of the world. People will always be moving and making new homes and friends. Most people will move several times in their lifetime.

Moving is a time of major change in a person's life.

Why do people move?

Families move for different reasons. Some are forced to move, while others choose to move.

Forced to move

Natural disasters can force families to move. Flash floods, or the occasional earthquake or tornado, can destroy homes and neighbourhoods. When homes are destroyed by natural disasters, some families are forced to move because they have lost everything they own.

Experiencing a natural disaster can be very scary. After a natural disaster, some families decide to move to a different location where the same natural disaster will not happen again. Moving after a disaster can be an especially difficult situation because people have usually lost everything they own. People who move after a natural disaster are often **resilient**. These people are able to move on with the support of family and friends.

Some families are forced to move after a natural disaster because their home and belongings are destroyed.

Case study

Jill was six when her house burned down. She remembers the pyjamas she was wearing when her parents picked her up out of bed and carried her from the house. Now 18 years old, Jill says that she didn't understand what was happening at the time. After the fire, she moved in with her grandma for a while. She remembers wanting a medal she won for reading books at school and feeling sad when she learned everything had been destroyed.

Family changes

Family changes can cause moves. Sometimes major events make moving necessary. If there is a death in the family, the remaining family members may move closer to **extended family**. Family members living close by can support and offer encouragement to those in need during difficult times of **grieving**.

When parents **divorce**, family members may move to live in different homes. It can be especially difficult to move during or after a sad time like a death or divorce.

Jobs are another reason that families may need to move. A parent may take a job in a different location. This often means that the whole family will move to the new area.

A family may have to move when a parent takes a new job.

NEWSFLASH

Currently the top three reasons people move are housing, family, and jobs. Sixty-two percent of families move for housing reasons. People want to own their own home and no longer rent. Some families want a different home or a home in a different neighbourhood. Twenty-five percent of people move to be closer to family, after divorce or death. Seven percent of people move to take new jobs or to commute shorter distances to work.

Grandchildren living close to grandparents can develop close **relationships**.

Choosing to move

Other families may choose to move. Some people want to move to a different neighbourhood. Families may move to a different neighbourhood where the crime rate is lower and they feel safer. Some families move into an area to be closer to better schools.

Wanting to live closer to grandparents or other relatives is another reason for a move. Living near relatives allows families to help each other. Families and friends who live close together can more easily maintain their **traditions**.

Military families on the move

Most military families move every two to four years. They pack, say goodbye to family and friends, and set off to another **assignment**. Military families may move within the same country or across the world. They can live on a **base** or in the community. Many military bases have people and resources to help families with the moving process. They can help with finding new schools, housing, and even lining up a buddy when a family arrives at their new home.

Children of military families move more often than children of civilian families.

There are many different reasons for moving. There are also many different feelings about moving. Feelings can range from happy, excited, **anxious**, or sad as the family prepares for the move. Although moving can also be a new and fresh beginning, change can be scary. At times like this, young people have many questions such as what will the new area be like and who will be their friends. It is important for young people to talk to an adult about their concerns.

What do you think?

Military families are often transferred every two years. Some people think frequent moves make people more open-minded about different cultures and people around the world. Other people think frequent moving causes stress because of constant changes. What do you think are the benefits of moving as often as military families?

Packing up and saying goodbye

Familiar surroundings

Living in the same home for a long time can give a feeling of being safe and secure. Knowing where things belong is being familiar with one's surroundings. Losing that sense of security after a move can be difficult and even scary.

Families who move have to find new ways of doing things. Going to new places means getting out a map and finding out how to get around. Families who move find new shops, libraries, and even places of worship. Meal times, bed times, and other daily **routines** may change often until families are settled in their new location. Moving takes patience until a new routine is set.

People who move learn from many new and different experiences. Moving can be an exciting time.

Moving means changing familiar routines and daily habits.

An address book can help people remember important contact information.

Saying goodbye

Good friends are people who know and enjoy each other's company. Friends have memories of good times spent together. Leaving behind a person you know well can be upsetting.

A person may feel like they are leaving a piece of themselves behind when they move. Moving can be harder for teenagers than very young children. Older children already in school and teenagers have developed friendships that can make moving even more difficult.

Saying goodbye can be tough, but there are things that can be done to make it easier. A memory book can be made of places people have gone and fun things people have done with friends. People who are moving can take photos of each room inside their home, as well as the outside. Then a photo album can be put together. These things will help people remember their old home.

Case study

Before Natalie moved, her friends threw a going away party. Everyone brought a photo of something they had done with Natalie. Each person shared her memory and put the photo in Natalie's "Good Friends Memory Box". When she felt lonely, Natalie took out her "Good Friends Memory Box". Looking at the photos helped her feel better.

Young people packing up their own belongings can make a move go more smoothly.

Sorting and packing

Sorting out belongings to move can seem **overwhelming**. It can be helpful to start with a plan. Begin with one part of the room, such as one drawer or the wardrobe. Sorting things into several piles can be helpful.

Packing similar things together will make unpacking quicker and easier. Labelling each box with what is in the box helps when it is time to unpack. Working together, families can make one pile of items to pack and take along, another of things to be thrown away, and one for items to be recycled.

Everyone has important items to take along. These things will be different for each person. People need to respect each other's important items.

Top tip

It is important to pack a bag containing all the things you will need on the journey to your new home. Pack special items that you don't want to be separated from. You should also pack items that you will need or want before the rest of your belongings arrive at your new home.

Recycle and donate

People can use moving as a time to recycle or donate things they no longer use. Some families gather up all of the unwanted items they don't need anymore and have a car boot sale. The profit from the sale can be used to explore the new area's museums, restaurants, or other attractions.

Used books and magazines can often be donated to libraries, schools, hospitals, or nursing homes. Friends or neighbourhood children may enjoy receiving outgrown toys. Old papers, plastic, and glass items can be recycled rather than thrown away. Recycling and donating are good ways to help others and save the planet.

Donating items is a good way to help other families in need.

How moving makes people feel

When people move, they may have many different feelings. People may feel happy and excited one day, but sad and unsure the next. This is normal during stressful times.

Someone who is **apprehensive** about the unknown may find it helpful to talk to parents and ask questions. Even parents and other siblings are sometimes unsure and nervous about a move. Families should take time to talk together.

Seeing a new home for the first time can be exciting.

Case study

When Marcus's parents told him that they were moving, he was sad but a little excited. When he saw his new bedroom for the first time, he was happy. On the wall, was his football team's logo. Marcus decided that he was not going to repaint it!

Feeling alone

When a family arrives at their new home, a person may feel homesick or lonely. A person can feel physically sick when they are homesick. Some people find looking at photos of family and friends helps them feel better. Talking together while sharing a meal can help a family feel more at home in a new place. Taking a walk through the new neighbourhood can be helpful for people to meet others living in the same area.

Feeling excited

Some people may see moving as a wonderful adventure. They are ready and excited to meet new friends when they arrive at their new home. Everyone is different and experiences different feelings.

Young people may feel unhappy and alone in their new home.

The Internet is a good place to find out information about things to do in a new area.

Attitude

It is important to keep a healthy **attitude** when a person is busy with all the activities of moving. There are many different things a person can do to keep a healthy outlook. Families can ask questions and share ideas about moving. Time spent reading books about moving can be helpful. Writing thoughts, feelings, and experiences about moving in a diary can help make for a smoother transition.

Humour helps people keep their spirits up when they are sad. Laughter helps in keeping a healthy attitude about moving. When a person keeps a positive attitude and a good sense of humour, things look brighter.

Worries

Moving to a new city, into a new home, and enrolling in a new school can be nerve-racking. But planning and doing a few extra things can help make the move easier.

Find out what the new community has to offer in the way of activities and clubs for young people. See if there are any sports teams in the area. Join a school sport's team. Practising and playing together is a great way to meet new friends. There are activity clubs that pupils can join at school. Drama, photography, or science clubs are great ways to meet people who share the same interests.

Organizing a school tour before the first day of class is a good way to meet teachers and learn how to get around the building.

Top tips

There are things you can do to learn more about your new school before the first day.

- Ask an adult to call the school office to organize a tour, meet your new teachers, and learn about your class timetable.
- Ask for a buddy, someone you can get to know before school starts and who can help you during your first week at the new school.
- Ask questions: When does the school term start? What are the school hours? What is the school canteen like?

17

Physical feelings

There are many physical feelings associated with moving. Keeping a healthy body during a move is just as important as keeping a healthy outlook.

There are many different ways to stay healthy during a move. While unpacking boxes, remember to stop and eat. It is important to eat complete, balanced meals while moving and unpacking. Drink plenty of water every day.

Healthy food choices are especially important for busy families. Wholegrain sandwiches, veggie sticks, and fresh fruits are good choices. Eating healthy meals and snacks will help people keep up their energy for moving and **adjusting** to new routines.

Eating healthy meals will help people feel good physically.

Outside activities are a great way to find out about a new area.

In your new environment

Exercise is important for a healthy lifestyle. Getting outside and starting to exercise helps a person to feel better and stay healthy. Walking, running, or cycling around the new neighbourhood are great ways to exercise and meet new friends at the same time.

Families can go exploring and find a new shopping centre. While walking around a big shopping centre, a person can exercise, meet new people, and shop all at the same time.

It is important to keep a normal routine. Going to bed, waking up, and exercising at a regular time can help people get used to their new surroundings.

NEWSFLASH

When exercising, your brain releases chemicals called **endorphins**. Endorphins make you feel happy. Exercising can be a life-long healthy choice for body and mind. Walking or running can be a fun way to see your new area and meet new people.

Being new and making friends

Living in a new area or part of the country can take some adjusting. Many places and things may be different from what you are used to. Different roads, streets, and bus stops will take time to learn. Different school start times, teachers, pupils, and classes will all take time to get used to.

Moving means change. It takes time to adjust and become comfortable with a life change. Some people **cope** with change more easily than other people. It helps to be patient with other family members when change is difficult for them. If change is hard for you, give yourself extra time to adjust.

Case study

John was sad when his parents told him that his mum had a new job offer in another area. He didn't want to leave his friends and school, but his mum told him this new job was a good opportunity. John's parents told him that there was a good school in their new city and even a football team he could join. John decided to be okay with the move.

It takes time to become comfortable in a new place.

Exploring a new city can be fun for the whole family.

Long-distance moves

Some families move and experience more than just a different house and school. Families who move to a **foreign** country will often experience a different language and culture.

Some families move to places that have a different climate. Different parts of the world experience different weather conditions. Long-distance moves such as these can involve more things to get used to.

In different parts of the world, people do things differently. Families may eat different foods at different meal times. New locations may have unfamiliar names for common items. For example, water fountain, drinking fountain, and bubbler are all different names for the same item – something a person can drink water from.

Being new at school

When you're the new pupil at school, you can plan ahead to fit in and make new friends. Arriving early enough helps to allow time to find classrooms, the canteen, and the toilets.

Be **confident** when you walk into the school building on the first day. Walk tall with shoulders back and wear a smile. People remember a lot about a new person from their first impression. Make sure to introduce yourself to teachers, and remember to look people in the eye when you introduce yourself.

Walk in to school with confidence even if you don't feel confident on the inside.

What do you think?

Many people suggest moving during the summer to fit in easily when a new school year begins. Others believe it is better to move during the school year when new pupils can start school and meet many new friends straight away. Do you think it is better to move in the summer or during the school year?

Case study

To meet new friends Dan tried out for the local youth football team. He went to practices before school started and made new friends. On the first day of school, Dan knew some of his classmates by name, and it really helped him to make new friends.

Making new friends

Moving can mean a fresh start for people. A fresh start means a chance to meet new people and make new friends. Meeting people requires effort on the new person's part. For some people it can be scary to introduce themselves and talk with people they have never met before.

Taking the first step and introducing yourself to a person in class or someone in the hallway takes courage. Fortunately, you don't have to do all of the talking. Friends are good listeners. Become friends by listening to what the other person says and asking questions about their hobbies or sports they enjoy. A first conversation can lead to the beginning of a new friendship.

a club at
ol to meet
le with the
interests
u.

You may be able to meet new friends at school or in your neighbourhood.

Meeting people

Meeting new friends can be challenging at times, but there are ways to make it easier. Remember that your **attitude** affects your thoughts and feelings about moving and making new friends. Keeping a positive attitude will make it easier for you to adjust.

Be nice to people! When people visit you, be interested in them and learn more about them. Smiling at people and making eye contact is a way to attract new friends. People like to be around positive and happy people. Learning to laugh at yourself and having fun is also important when meeting new people.

Be yourself

When meeting new people, trust your gut feelings. If someone seems like a person you could be friends with, work at it. Share ideas, stories, and maybe even lunch to get to know that person. Be honest, and be yourself. People will enjoy being around you. New friends don't happen overnight.

Remember to keep in touch with friends from your old school and neighbourhood. If you're feeling lonely, the support of old friends can be comforting. If you are having trouble adjusting to a new place and making friends, a **counsellor** can be a helpful person to talk to. Many schools have counsellors who are able to help new pupils adjust.

Joining a sports team is a good way to meet new friends.

Top tips

Here are some tips for meeting new people and making friends:

- Smile when you meet people.
- Introduce yourself to people you have not met before.
- Remember the names of new friends.
- Behave confidently while talking to people.
- Be yourself!

Staying in touch

Staying in touch with old friends is important. After moving to a new location, people need the support of close friends more than ever. Many people want to stay in touch with friends, but it is hard to find time. People are busy with school, sports, and after-school activities. It is important to make time to stay in touch with friends.

Ways to keep in touch

There are many different ways friends can stay in touch. Email is a quick and easy way to stay in touch. You can email old friends to tell them what is happening in your new home. Talking on the phone or even texting can also help. Friends can use their imaginations when it comes to staying in touch by making a video, sending artwork, or starting a newspaper of events.

People change and grow, but friends always have the memories of the fun times they spent together.

Many people consider moving to be one of life's most stressful events. Leaving behind friends, familiar places, and well-known activities creates anxiety for everyone in the family, even parents.

Moving to a new location may take some adjusting. Adjusting to a new home, neighbourhood, and school can all take time. Stay in touch with old friends and keep a positive **attitude**. Soon you will make new friends and become familiar with your surroundings. Moving doesn't have to be a challenge. It can be a life adventure.

Technology makes it easier for people to stay in touch.

Top tips

There are many ways to stay in touch with people.
- Set aside a special time that works for you and your friend to ring each other.
- Send texts or emails with your new address and information to friends and family.
- Take a holiday back to your old town or city and visit old friends.
- Invite your old friends for a visit and introduce them to your new friends.

Facts about moving

- People over the age of 65 have on average moved 5.7 times in their life. However, 18–25-year-olds have moved more than 3 times since they left their parents' house.

- Young people today are likely to move more than twice as many times as their grandparents.

- The August Bank Holiday weekend is one of the most popular times to move house because there is an extra day off work for adults, it's the school holidays, and the weather is good.

- 196,000 British people left the UK to live abroad in the year up to mid-2006.

- Every year more than 2,500 pets are relocated for families around the world.

- Moving can be one of the most stressful events in a person's life.

- Moving can be hardest on teenagers.

- It is common to experience many different emotions when moving.

- A positive attitude helps when moving and meeting new people.

- Communication is very important when moving.

Glossary

adjusting getting used to a change

anxious nervous and upset

apprehensive worried and slightly afraid

assignment job given to someone

attitude opinions and feelings about someone or something

attracted interested in

base place from which a branch of the armed services is controlled

climate usual weather of a certain place

confident having a strong belief in your own abilities

cope deal with

counsellor someone who is trained to help people with their problems

culture way of life of a group of people

divorce end a marriage

endorphin substance produced by the brain and used by the body

extended family members of a family other than parents and siblings

famine time when there is not enough food for everyone

foreign something that is different or unfamiliar

grieving feeling extremely sad about the death of a loved one

natural disaster severe weather or other dangerous occurrence in nature

overwhelming feeling of having too much to do or too much to handle at one time

relationship way in which people get on with each other

resilient ability to recover from bad situations

routine usual habits and way of life

stressful worrying and difficult

tradition belief and custom followed by a group of people

Further resources

Moving is a time of major change. If you are dealing with a move, remember that you aren't alone. As well as your family and friends, there are many resources available to help you cope with moving.

Books

Moving People: Migration and Settlement, Louise Spilsbury
    (Heinemann-Raintree, 2006)
 An introduction to the effects of migration.

People on the Move: Environmental Migrants, Dave Dalton (Heinemann, 2005)
This book explores the reasons why people migrate.

Tough Trivia for Kids: An Official Mensa Puzzle Book, Helene Hovanec
    (Sterling Juvenile, 2006)
Make the journey to the new house go faster with some tough trivia quizzes.

Websites

Childline
www.childline.org.uk/ContactChildLine.asp
Contact details for Childline are on this page. They can help with whatever problems you may have.

Moving pets
www.directline.com/pet/moving_house.htm
On this web page you can find tips on moving your pet and helping it to adjust to a new home.

Websites (continued)

Puzzle games
http://thinks.com/puzzles/
On this website you can print off many different puzzles to take with you on the journey to the new home. They include sudoku, riddles, anagrams, picture puzzles, trivia, and maths puzzles.

Samaritans
www.samaritans.org/talk_to_someone.aspx
The Samaritans are there to help whatever your problem. This web page gives you all the contact details.

Organization

The Salvation Army
615 Slaters Lane
P.O. Box 269
Alexandria, Virginia 22313
Website: www.salvationarmy.org
The Salvation Army accepts many kinds of donations, such as clothing and household items.

Index